Feeling All My Grief

Kim T. S.

In memory of Kong Kong Hen
on the fourth anniversary of his death

February 1, 1954 to August 27, 2019
"Family first."

I love you, daddy.
Thank you for everything.
♡ Kim

For loved ones gone too soon,
and hearts that miss them dearly.

Dear Reader,

My dad had a massive heart attack when my son was three years old. I hugged him and whispered: "Grandpa died, and we'll miss him dearly. We're lucky to have so many beautiful memories of him. He will always be in our hearts."

At the age of five, he started worrying about how we'd all die one day. "I understand. It's normal to worry about death. Even grown-ups do. But we need to remember that it's a normal part of life. Every day, people die. And every day, babies are born, too!
We can't predict the future, but we can make the most of the present. So let's create wonderful memories and treasure our time together! No matter what happens, I will always be in your heart."

It's important to be truthful when talking to kids about death, and it will likely take several conversations throughout the years. You know your children best, so do what feels right to you.

I hope this book helps you discuss grief with your little ones.

 Kim

This book belongs to:

____

It's truly hard to cope when
someone dear to you has died.
You won't want to believe it,
seeking answers far and wide.

Some people want to cry it out.
I've felt the same way, too.
And when it leaves you so confused,
what can you say . . . or do?

Why did they have to go and die?
And are they truly gone?
It's something that I can't accept.
I really can't move on!

Now, here's a name for what we feel:
This heavy weight is grief.
A painful loss can dig so deep,
it's hard to find relief.

But grief can show its face to us
in many different ways.
At times, you'll want to be alone—
and long for quiet days.

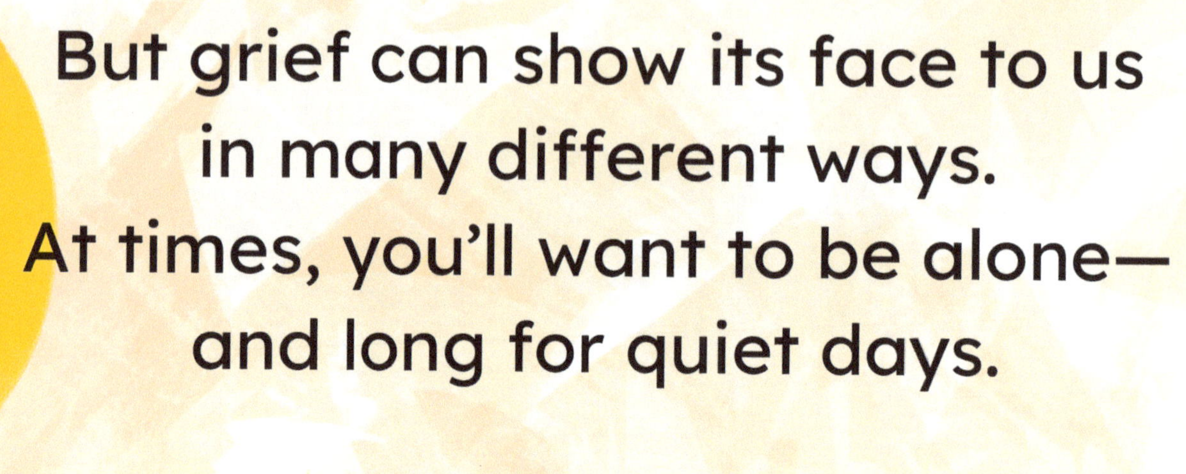

Some people like to be around
their family and friends,
while others try to have some fun.
It really all depends!

Your grief can be a mix of feelings:
anger, sadness, fear.
Then worry may come knocking, too,
but that's alright, my dear.

Now, if you feel a few of these,
or even none at all,
know what you feel is valid—
whether seeming big or small.

Please take your time to feel it all,
but look for shining rays.
You'll find a light within your heart
and have much brighter days.

The sadness won't completely fade.
Yet, soon you'll make some space
for gratitude and happiness
and love to take its place.

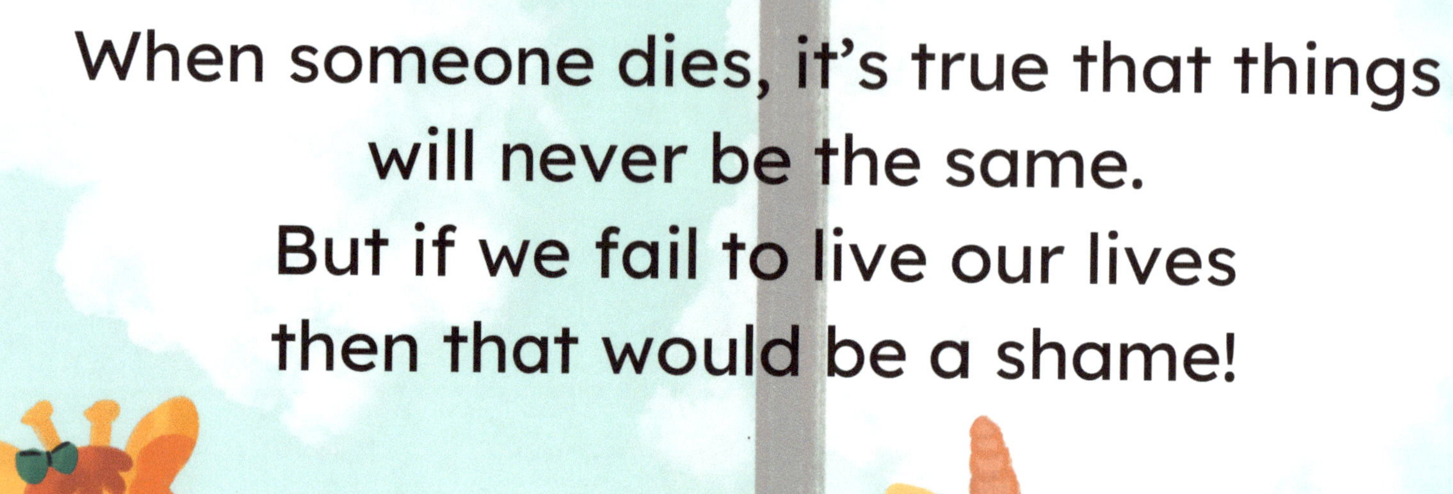

When someone dies, it's true that things
will never be the same.
But if we fail to live our lives
then that would be a shame!

They may be gone, but we'll make sure
their memories won't fade.
A part of them ignites our hearts.
How strong our love was made!

The simple joys can matter most:
Time spent with love and care.
Oh, let's not focus on the end . . .
We've moments left to share!

The special journey of your life
has only just begun.
So come and hug me for a while –
I love you, little one.

If our books have helped you in any way, please let us know! Review us on amazon and Goodreads:

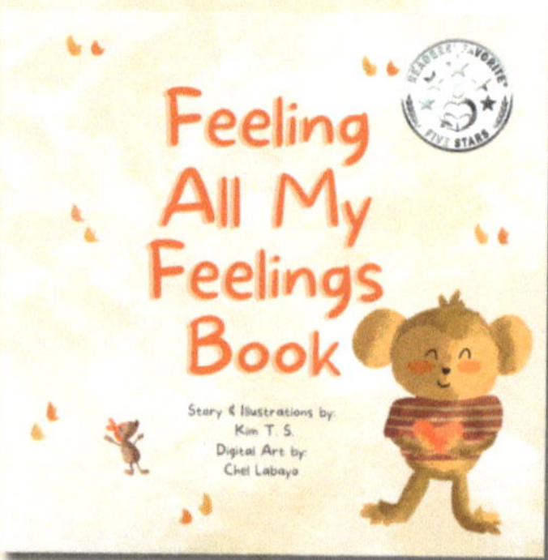

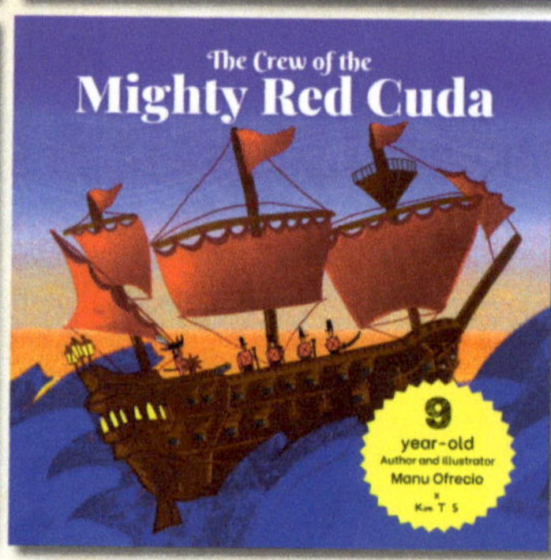

Your feedback inspires us to keep writing.

Want freebies?

Get FREE emotional regulation activity sheets through our mailing list. Use your smartphone camera to scan the code below, then tap the link. Or visit our website!

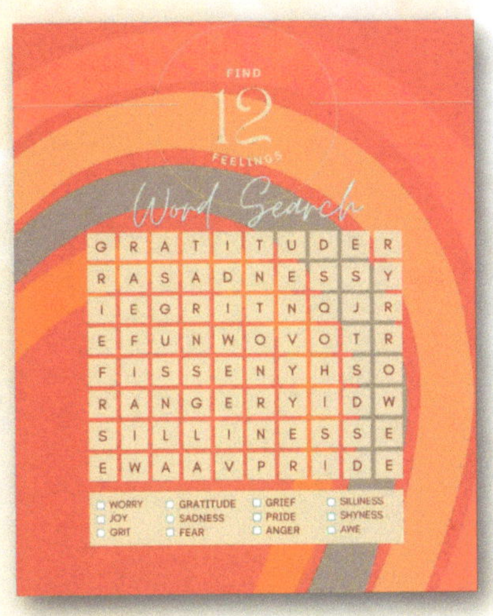

@kimt.s.books - @kimtsbooks - kimtsbooks@gmail.com

www.kimtsbooks.com

Write a letter or draw a picture for your loved one.

The lessons we learn from them stay with us.
What are the best things they taught you?
(If you never met them, or if you were too little to
remember, that's okay. Their memories live on through
the stories we hear about them.)

Place your favorite photos here.

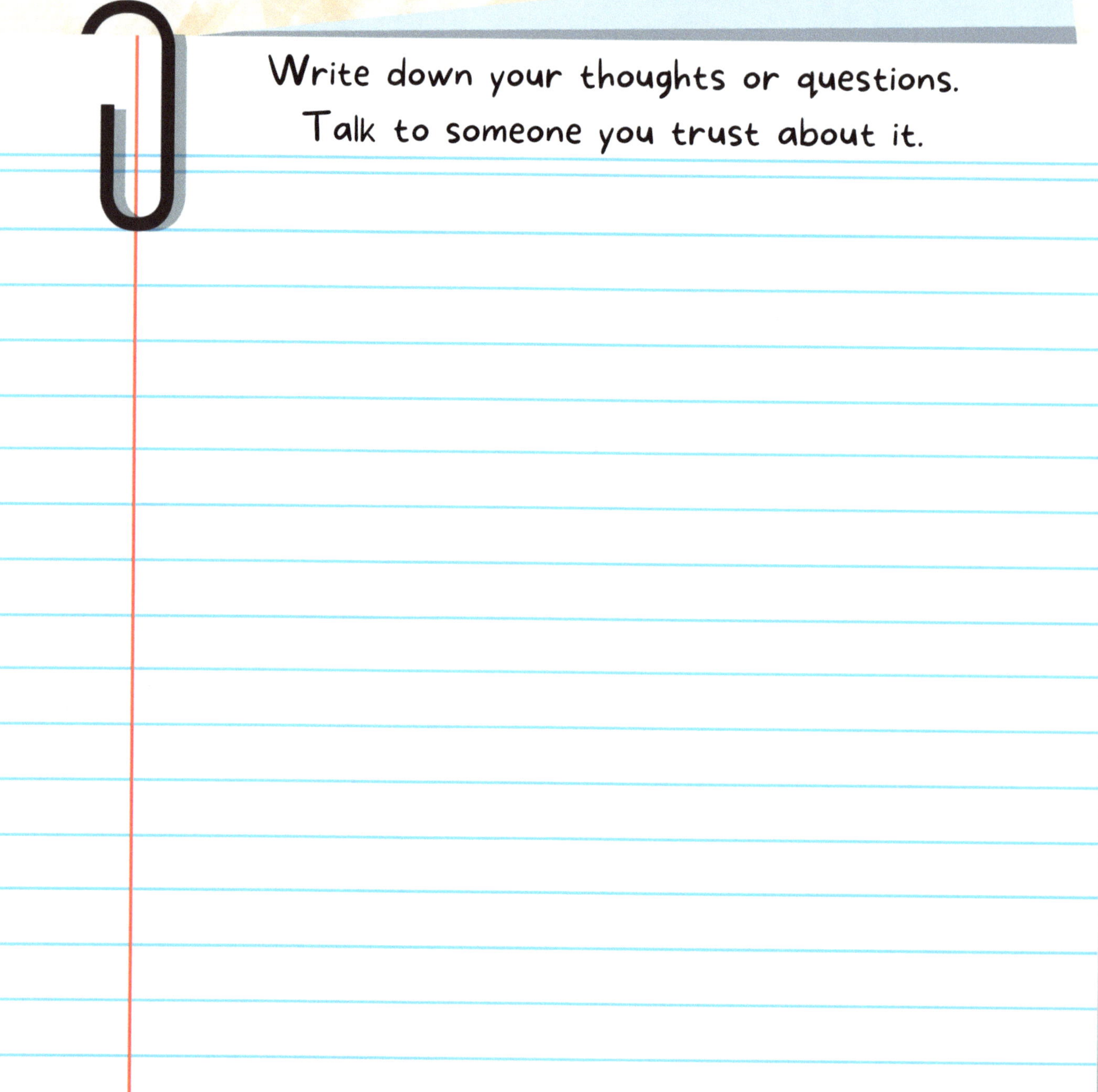

Write down your thoughts or questions.
Talk to someone you trust about it.

What memories are you looking forward to making, and with who? Tell them about it!

Have you seen grown-ups having a hard time? What did you notice? Did you feel responsible for their feelings or think that it's your fault?

Grown-ups can also have a hard time dealing with grief and other big feelings. Just like you, they may need some time to process them.

Other people's feelings are not your responsibility, and how they feel or act is not your fault. But we should always find ways to be kind and help each other.

No matter how hard it feels, you are strong enough to get through it.

Ideas for coping with grief:

Plant a tree

Create a memory book

Let out your feelings

Talk to a grown-up you trust

Lots of hugs

What are your ideas?

Send us a photo of this or tag us on social media @kimt.s.books - your ideas might help someone!